Driving On Motorways

Fully Instructional

by

Greeny

Bloomington, IN  Milton Keynes, UK

AuthorHouse™
1663 Liberty Drive, Suite 200
Bloomington, IN 47403
www.authorhouse.com
Phone: 1-800-839-8640

AuthorHouse™ UK Ltd.
500 Avebury Boulevard
Central Milton Keynes, MK9 2BE
www.authorhouse.co.uk
Phone: 08001974150

© 2007 Greeny. All rights reserved.

No part of this book may be reproduced, stored in a retrieval system, or transmitted by any means without the written permission of the author.

First published by AuthorHouse 2/19/2007

ISBN: 1-4259-3253-3 (sc)

Printed in the United States of America
Bloomington, Indiana

This book is printed on acid-free paper.

INTRODUCTION

This book is aimed mainly at the inexperienced driver having recently passed their test, but it is also an ideal way for any driver wishing to drive on our Motorways to

Get a full understanding on how to use them safely. When we want to learn how to drive on our major "A" roads we go to a Driving Instructor, take lessons, and we are taught how to drive in a safe and proper manner, then we take the Government's driving test, after passing, we can then drive on any Motorway without taking any tuition what so ever and just take pot luck as to how we get on, I know that some drivers do take a few Motorway lessons and some take Pass Plus to get more experience and cheaper insurance but that is no where near enough tuition for Motorways and this is where the trouble lies. New drivers who have not taken any tuition for Motorway driving think they know how to drive safely on Motorways but because they have not been taught they find it a completely different kettle of fish and that applies to a lot of experienced drivers too.

Motorways first started creeping up on us when back in 1958 the first stretch was opened as the Preston Bypass in Lancashire. Following that, over the years we now have a very good network of Motorways covering most of the country That is a good thing but wait, do we know how to drive on them safely? Motorway driving requires a very high level of driving skills and awareness because of high speeds and volume of traffic which means that dangerous situations develop much more quickly, using Motorways enables you to drive faster over long distances than when on ordinary roads because there are no sharp bends, steep hills, traffic lights, or ordinary road junctions to deal with, plus the fact that all the traffic is flowing in the same direction so really we could not have a safer stretch of road to drive on than a Motorway. Driving at high speeds for long periods of time makes concentration, observation, patience and anticipation very important factors the greater the volume of traffic, the greater the demand of your attention and decision making. Most books that you read about Motorway driving only give you a short chapter about it but if you take the time to read this book completely you will find that it will take you on a complete Motorway journey from start to finish explaining exactly how to complete that journey safely. A full explanation of what the book comprises of, the need for it and why I have decided to do a complete journey on a Motorway.

CONTENTS

CHAPTER ONE   FITNESS OF THE DRIVER 1

Explains the importance of how fit and fresh a driver should be to be able to drive safely and the importance of not driving when under the influence of medication or alcohol.

CHAPTER TWO   CONDITION OF YOUR VEHICLE 5

Explains the importance of good maintenance of your vehicle especially on Motorways.

CHAPTER THREE   PLANNING YOUR JOURNEY 9

Explains the importance of planning your journey before starting out.

CHAPTER FOUR   JOINING THE MOTOR WAY 13

Explains in detail how to join the Motorway safely.

CHAPTER FIVE   TIME AND SPACE 19

Explains the importance of giving your driving plenty of time and space, time to make your manoeuvres and space to do them in.

CHAPTER SIX   FOLLOWING AND STOPPING DISTANCES 25

Explains the dangers in following other traffic too close, also keeping your distance.

CHAPTER SEVEN   LANE DISCIPLINE............ 31

Explains the importance of correct lane changing.

CHAPTER EIGHT   OVERTAKING AND
       MAKING PROGRESS.. 37

Explains how to overtake safely on a Motorway, also the importance of making good progress.

CHAPTER NINE   APPROACHING JUNCTIONS
       AND SERVICE AREAS 45

Explains the traffic pattern changes and the dangers involved when approaching these areas.

CHAPTER TEN   DEALING WITH ROAD-
       WORKS 51

Explains how to drive through road works safely.

CHAPTER ELEVEN   DRIVING IN ADVERSE
       WEATHER CONDITIONS................................ 55

Explains the importance of adjusting your driving in bad weather.

CHAPTER TWELVE   DRIVING AT NIGHT 63

Describes the difference between day and night driving.

CHAPTER THIRTEEN   BREAKDOWNS ON
       MOTORWAYS 67

How to deal with break downs on Motorways

CHAPTER FOURTEEN   LEAVING THE
    MOTORWAY.. 73

Explains how to leave the Motorway safely.

CHAPTER ONE
FITNESS OF THE DRIVER

Driving when you are ill is not recommended on any roads let alone Motorways as the slightest illness can impair your ability behind the wheel. Even a bad nights sleep can be enough to affect your concentration, so when you are ill, only you can decide whether you are fit to drive, and if you must drive then you must take extra care. Being under the Doctor and taking medication can be as dangerous as driving under the influence of alcohol in your system and we should all know by now how dangerous it is to mix driving and alcohol together so if you are prescribed any kind of medication you must check with your Doctor before driving. The extra concentration needed and the high speeds and some times long distances travelled on Motorways means

Fully Instructional

that it is more essential than usual to ensure that you are in good health.

Have a good rest before starting your journey, as a well rested mind makes you feel fit and fresh and it enables you to concentrate clearly and think positively, far better than a tired mind would do. Try to wear some loose fitting clothes for your comfort on the journey as there is nothing worse than sitting behind the wheel for maybe hours getting discomfort from tight fitting clothes, if this is the case your discomfort is distracting your mind from doing its job of concentrating on your driving.

Wearing the correct footwear is also very important, the ideal footwear for driving is a pair of light, thin soled shoes because the thin soles allow your feet to feel and operate the pedals more easily as thick soled shoes such as trainers are not ideal because your feet feel clumsy and you can't feel the pedals so well because of the thick soles (nothing wrong with trainers as I think they are very smart to wear but I do not recommend them for driving in). You should also make sure that your eyesight meets the required standard by law, which can be found in your current Highway Code. Avoid eating a heavy meal before starting out as this can make you feel drowsy, and if this is the case wind your window down slightly to get some fresh air circulating to freshen you up and then stop at the next Service Area to take some rest as fatigue can be a killer.

CHAPTER TWO
CONDITION OF YOUR VEHICLE

Before we talk about the condition of the vehicle, for the purpose of this journey, for simplicity, lets assume that we are driving in an ordinary family saloon car on a three lane Motorway. The contents of this book applies to all drivers using Motorways. The condition of your vehicle to drive on any road must be in very good roadworthy condition, not only for your own safety but for the safety of all other road users as the law demands. The conditions of Motorway driving creates a greater demand from your vehicle as you will probably be driving for longer periods of time at greater speeds so therefore you need a vehicle which can stand up to these conditions. Now lets look at the things you should

Fully Instructional

be sure of before starting out, its very important that you take the time to carry out these checks as it can be very expensive to be towed off the Motorway by breakdown vehicles as repairs cannot be carried out by yourself on the hard shoulder, minor repairs may be carried out by the recovery people on the hard shoulder but mainly it's a tow job at your expense so this is why I cannot emphasise too much the importance of always having a well maintained vehicle.

First of all you must make sure that you check your oil, water and fuel because if you run short of any of these fluids you may find that sometimes it can be a very long way to the next Service Area. The next check is your tyre pressures, not forgetting your spare-wheel, as this wheel plays a very important part in that if you get a puncture or a blow out, when you go to get the spare wheel its lying there in your boot flat then it does not help things at all. If a vehicle, especially a fully loaded one is travelling at high speeds with incorrect tyre pressures the driver has not got full control of the vehicle's handling ability not to mention breaking the law. I would also like to mention the fact that tyres that are below their recommended pressures overheat and that can cause blowouts which is a common cause of accidents.

You must also make sure that your tyres have the required tread depth to obtain maximum grip to the road surface, the legal requirements that the law states can be found in your current edition of the Highway Code which all drivers should be in possession of and should all be familiar with. The windscreen wipers should be in working order and you should check the rubber blades to make sure that they wipe the windscreen cleanly, especially at night and don't forget to check the washers, not forgetting to top up the washer bottle.

The heater must also be in good working order because you not only need to keep warm in adverse weather conditions, in some situations you may also need cool air circulating around the car to keep the windows from steaming up and obscuring your vision as there is nothing more important when driving than having good all round vision. Your steering and brakes should be working correctly, a good way to check your brakes is to do what we call a rolling break check, that is, before starting any journey, drive the vehicle off and at about 20 mph try the brakes, making sure there is no other driver close behind before you do, only start your journey if they are working correctly. If you have a roof rack fitted to your vehicle make sure that it is well secured, and any luggage that you may have in it is also well secured for the journey. All lights, including

Fully Instructional

indicators and brake lights must all be working with no cracked lenses, seat belts must be in good working order and you must make sure that your head restraints are correctly adjusted to prevent whip-lash should you be unfortunate enough to be involved in an accident. Last but not least you must check that the insurance has not expired, the road fund licence is valid and that the vehicle has an M.O.T. certificate if one is required.

CHAPTER THREE
PLANNING YOUR JOURNEY

Making any journey is less stressful if you plan it first, especially if you travel by Motorway. One very important point I would like to mention about Motorway journeys is that if you have a very important appointment that can't be missed under any circumstances at your destination, I do not recommend you using a Motorway at all. The reason for this is that if anything unfortunate should happen which would mean closing the Motorway, you can only join and leave at a Motorway junction, so lets say that there is an accident, all traffic slows down and stops, depending on the severity of the accident you may have to sit and wait for an hour or so until the carriageway is cleared and remember you will be

Fully Instructional

somewhere between two junctions not being able to do anything about it so bang goes your appointment, another very important point to take into consideration is that if you suffer from Diabetes, when your blood sugars run low you have to eat to stop yourself from having an hypoglycaemic attack so I would recommend always carrying a pack of digestive biscuits in your car to cover any situations. If you were to be using major "A" roads and the road becomes blocked you can at least turn round and divert on to other roads but not on a Motorway.

I have mentioned this early in this chapter because this is a very important factor to bear in mind when planning your journey, otherwise use the Motorways, give yourself plenty of time and go for it. Get plenty of rest before you start and then you will feel fit and fresh and ready to face the task. You first look at the route map to find out which are the major "A" roads you will use to get you to the Motorway that you will want to use first. Its important to do this because if you don't and you get lost before you find your first Motorway junction, chances are that you will find yourself becoming stressed out before you even start your Motorway journey. On major "A" roads you can usually stop somewhere safe to check your map but once you are on the Motorway there is no stopping on

Driving On Motorways

the hard shoulder as that is for emergencies only and the next Service Area may be miles away so you can see the importance of good forward planning. I will be talking about the hard shoulder later on in the book.

All Motorways have different numbers to identify them by, for example M.1. M.5. M 6. And so on and all the Motorway junctions are numbered as you will see on your map so all you have to do is write down the number of the junction you will be entering by. Follow the Motorway as you may have to use more than one to get to your destination depending on where you are going until you find the junction that you need to leave the Motorway by. Write the numbers down especially your exit number and its as easy as that. You may not be used to driving for long periods of time so make sure that you put some rest periods in as fatigue can be a killer.

Driving for long periods of time brings on tiredness which in turn greatly increases your accident risk so allow yourself plenty of time. I will be talking about the importance of time later as it plays such an important part in safe driving. A very good tip to remember is that every time you see a Service Area sign always check your fuel and decide whether you have enough for the journey or do you need to stop. A well planned journey should turn out to be a good journey because

Fully Instructional

you know exactly what you are doing, in turn that gives you satisfaction so that it is not just a task to get from A to B you will find that you actually enjoyed it.

CHAPTER FOUR
JOINING THE MOTORWAY

Before setting out on any journey, we must make sure that we are comfortable with the vehicle that we are going to drive, For example you may have borrowed your friend's car or hired one so we must make sure that we fit into it comfortably.

Before getting into the car, make an external inspection by walking round the vehicle to see if there is anything broken or hanging off, a number for example also check for a flat tyre. This is a very good habit to get your self into as it could possibly save you a lot of trouble further down the road, if the vehicle that you are going to use for this journey is not your usual one then you must familiarise yourself with that vehicle and what I mean by that is you must find out where

Fully Instructional

the controls are in your new car because different cars sometimes position the controls in different places and its just not safe to be searching round the dash board looking for a particular control after you have started to drive because this is just not safe so you must do this before you start to drive. Once we have familiarised our self with the controls we then carry out the cockpit drill, this will be familiar with all new drivers as they would have to do this at the start of every lesson they would take with their Driving Instructor.

First of all make sure that all doors are securely closed we have all been overtaken by cars with a door not properly closed imagine the dangers of that with children sitting on the back seat. Then we check the seating position to make sure that we can reach the pedals easily, we should not have to stretch to reach the pedals nor should we be too near, think of a long journey being bunched up too near to the controls, not being able to use them comfortably, this would be a big distraction from your driving so it is important that we take the time to carry out this drill, some of us are short and some of us are tall so we all need different driving positions. To find out our own comfortable seating position we would depress the clutch pedal fully and slide the seat forwards or backwards as the case may be

Driving On Motorways

until we have a slight bend in the left knee which will allow us to press the pedal without having to stretch.

Remember to adjust the head restraints correctly for whiplash in the unfortunate event of an accident.

We then check the steering wheel, to steer comfortably and safely we should have a slight bend at the elbows, again not stretching to reach it, you will see that everything points towards comfort, as the more comfortable you are behind the wheel the safer your driving will be. Next we make sure that all our mirrors are correctly adjusted so that we can obtain good all round vision, not only to the rear but down both sides of the car as there is nothing more important when driving than having good all round vision. Check the foot brake for firmness and the handbrake for tension also not forgetting to check that the windscreen wipers and washers are working. We have discussed the rest of the checks in the previous chapter, not forgetting to fasten all seat belts and checking your fuel for the journey and making sure that all windows are clean inside and out. We are now ready for the journey, carry out a rolling brake check and you are now ready to start your journey To join the Motorway we usually use a slip road which enables us to match our speed to the traffic on the Motorway and merge with it safely. Slip roads usually start from a roundabout above the

Fully Instructional

Motorway, so that when you enter the slip road and pass the official Motorway sign you then come under Motorway regulations which means that you can't stop on the hard shoulder for any reason other than an emergency or instructed to stop by the Police, you can't set down or pick up any passengers until you have left the Motorway. From the roundabout you are in a good elevated position which allows you to see how the traffic is flowing, slip roads usually have two lanes for entering and leaving the Motorways with, I strongly recommend that you stay in the nearside lane to enter the carriage because you have then got everything on your right hand side which then makes the task of merging easier so you don't have to concentrate on your left because you know that there is nothing there.

If you decide to use the offside lane of the slip road you have not only got to concentrate on the Motorway traffic but you have also got to think about the drivers on your left in the nearside lane which then makes the task of merging twice as difficult especially when you both arrive at the point of merging it can be very hazardous so the golden rule is always keep to the left if possible. When leaving the Motorway the lane you select on the slip road obviously depends on the direction you are taking. Some slip roads continue into an extra lane on the main carriageway, if this is the case stay in

Driving On Motorways

that lane until you have adjusted yourself to the higher speeds. A good driver always makes the task of driving as easy and as safely as possible by forward planning, merging is just one good example of it. So, when we are travelling along the slip road in the near side lane displaying a good clear right hand signal we start to look for a safe gap in the traffic on the carriageway, we must remember that this traffic has got priority and we must never cause other road users to slow down or worst of all stop so we must always give way to it, we must never force our way in because if you do, just think of all the interruption you cause to the traffic on the carriageways having to brake or change lanes and don't forget this interruption causes a chain reaction which goes all the way back down the carriageway and if the traffic flow is heavy this can be very dangerous indeed so remember to give way.

Once we have found a safe gap we then adjust our speed to match the speed of the Motorway traffic, making sure that our blind spot is clear we merge smoothly and safely on to the carriageway in lane one never merge straight into lane two as that is just not safe because the traffic pattern changes so quickly that you can't make sure that both lanes are clear at the same time, always lane one first. Stay in lane one until you have adjusted yourself to the higher speeds before moving out. Your

Fully Instructional

blind spot is the area that you can't see into when you are checking your mirrors so you have to physically look into that area yourself to make sure it is clear as another driver could be sitting there, a motor cyclist for example as they can sometimes be very difficult to see, this is a good thing to remember ourselves never to drive in other people's blind spots. A shoulder check means that we look to our right or left as the case may be but only to see if it is clear, only check to shoulder level never look back whilst we are driving especially at high speeds as it is far too dangerous we only look back over our shoulder when we are moving off from stationary. If when merging the traffic is very heavy you may find it difficult to get in straight away it is better to use a short stretch of the hard shoulder until someone lets you in than stopping altogether because joining a Motorway from stationary can be very dangerous but we will talk about that later in the book.

CHAPTER FIVE
TIME AND SPACE

Time and space are two of the most important words in driving today, impatience is a very big accident factor. The reason why there are usually so many vehicles involved in Motorway accidents is because drivers simply drive too close to each other, when an accident occurs the vehicles following immediately behind the accident vehicles cannot stop, they just simply have not got time to stop nor have they Time and space are two of the most important words in driving today impatience is got any space to stop in. They suddenly find themselves with nowhere to go so they just pile in to each other and that is why we see so much carnage on the Motorways today. When driving on any road we must always be looking as far ahead as possible and acting upon what

Fully Instructional

we see, keeping a good following distance from the vehicle in front, the need for forward planning when driving on

Motorways becomes even more so because of the high speeds and volume of traffic.

When we are scanning the horizon ahead and see the odd brake light come on now and then we don't give it too much thought but if we see all the brake lights coming on in all the lanes and staying on that is a very good indication that there is trouble ahead and traffic could either be slowing down or stopping so that gives you plenty of time to react to what you are seeing.

Motorways are the safest roads to drive on because they are mainly straight stretches of road and all the traffic is going in the same direction with no roundabouts, sharp bends, traffic lights etc to deal with but drivers have still not adjusted themselves to using them in a safe and proper manner. A few new drivers have taken Motorway training but not many because as any Driving Instructor will tell you Motorway lessons are hard to sell to pupils, cost of extra training being the main factor plus the fact that Motorway training still remains optional to the new driver so the majority of them start out in their driving careers learning how to cope with Motorway driving through trial and error the same as a lot of drivers do.

Driving On Motorways

Many drivers will tell you that dad will take me on the Motorway, nothing wrong with that, but does dad know how to use a Motorway correctly. If say six Motorway lessons were to become mandatory after passing the driving test then Motorways would be much safer places to drive on obviously this would exclude advanced drivers because as I said earlier I am aiming this book at the new driver and Mrs and Mr average driver. If we all had training to use Motorways the same as we had to use ordinary roads it would save this country millions of pounds in the National Health Service and the Emergency Services not to mention the human misery side of it.

As new drivers, just starting out in your driving careers if you follow the advice given, as your experience builds up you will see how time and space fits in and how much safer your driving will become, for example, before making any manoeuvre where a signal is required, give a good clear and early signal of your intentions before moving out, that will give all other road users time to react to your manoeuvre because they have plenty of warning of your intentions which makes driving much easier and safer, plus the fact that it will help to reduce your stress levels. Putting plenty of time and space practise into your driving, you never know, you might actually enjoy it. Attitudes play a very

Fully Instructional

important part in safe driving, you may not be aware of it but you display your frame of mind in your driving, if for instance you got up this morning feeling fit and fresh after a good nights sleep, on your way into your place of work you would be more inclined to take your time with your driving, giving way to other drivers, giving your overtaking manoeuvres more time and attention simply because you are in a good frame of mind and you are feeling good with yourself.

On the other hand if the opposite were to be true, you are late up for work, you have just had words with your wife or children, you have just received a large bill in the post, how will your driving be today on your way in to work?. You will not feel like giving way so much and letting other drivers in, your driving may be much faster because you are in a bad mood, you will not be giving your overtaking manoeuvres hardly any attention at all because your mind is not focussed on your driving. Your accident risk levels are rising rapidly, this just shows you how attitudes play such a big part in safe driving. If for example you have any major upsets in your life such as a death or anything of that nature you should not be driving on any roads at all let alone Motorways because your mind is full of other things and you just can't concentrate on your driving 100%. Just imagine driving along giving your driving

Driving On Motorways

no attention at all, what a danger you are, not only to yourself but to all other road users, so my advise is, if you are not in the right frame of mind to drive then leave it until tomorrow or get someone else to drive for you, you may live longer. If anything goes wrong and it seems to be your fault what is the first thing the other person says to you, why were you not looking at what you were doing, didn't you see me coming.

CHAPTER SIX
FOLLOWING AND STOPPING DISTANCES

In the last chapter we talked about time and space, now we are going to talk about following and stopping distances, and you will now see how this chapter reinforces the importance of time and space. When following other traffic, in the unfortunate event of an accident or emergency, when all the traffic comes to a stop, you must always leave yourself enough time to stop and very importantly enough space to stop in. This applies to all roads not just Motorways, think that this has just got to make sense and I think you must agree with me on this, so we have got to ask ourselves why do we do the opposite and drive too close to each other. At the risk of repeating myself this is why when

Fully Instructional

on a Motorway an accident happens how many times on the media do you hear about a accident on such and such Motorway with say 50 or 60 vehicles involved we can now see why they are so big simply because drivers have not got time to stop or enough space to stop in. Drivers always drive far too close to each other and when the accident happens they have nowhere to go so they smash into the vehicle in front of them and that is such a shame because all this can be avoided by simply keeping your correct following distance from the vehicle in front of you. If you read your current Highway Code you will see that, travelling at 70mph you will need at least 96 metres to stop in and that's a long way you might think but that is in good driving conditions when the road is dry and clean but when the roads are wet you need at least double that distance to stop in and when there is snow and ice about you can increase that distance even further because your tyres just can't grip the road surface and get you stopped in time. An easy guide to remember about following distances is to keep a distance between you and the vehicle in front of you is roughly a metre for each mile per hour travelled, that gives us our minimum overall stopping distance in good road and traffic conditions. If we know that we have got to stop we should check our mirrors to see what is happening to the rear and both

Driving On Motorways

sides of our vehicle and then start to brake early and progressively, as we all know when we start to brake our brake lights come on, these brake lights serve a very important purpose because they are a signal to all other road users telling them that we are either slowing down or stopping. If we start to brake early and give a good clear signal with our brake lights to all other road users that we are slowing down or stopping they have got time to do the same and in this way we get a chain reaction back down the carriageway so that everyone knows what we are doing. This way we have all got time to stop and space to stop in so there is no need for us all to go smashing into each other. We hear people saying that an accident happened, most of the time accidents don't just happen they are caused by driver error, driving too fast for road and traffic conditions and too close.

Is it becoming clear yet how important time and space is?. Another very good reason why we should not drive too close to vehicles in front of us is that our view to the front is severely restricted especially if we are behind Large Goods Vehicles (L.G.V.s) and coaches.

We should always keep back and use our overall stopping distance from the vehicles in front especially coaches and L.G.V.s as the further we drive behind them the better the view we can get to the front as we are able to see down both sides of them so if you are

Fully Instructional

considering an overtaking manoeuvre it helps to make your decision making easier, can we see where abiding by the rules and driving sensibly it makes driving so much easier not to mention safer. An easy way to get a picture of what your overall stopping distance looks like is to pick any road sign on the Motorway and as the vehicle in front of you passes that sign say to yourself (only a fool breaks the two second rule) and if you pass that sign before you have finished saying it then drop back because you are too close, that is what we call the two second rule and if we add our thinking and braking distances together we need at least two seconds to stop safely in, that is when road conditions are good.

We should always be able to stop safely well within the distance we can see to be clear ahead. A few words now about mobile phones, I am a great believer in the mobile phone as they now make communication so much easier by their convenience but they do not fit in with your driving, especially on Motorways. When you know that you are going to be using your car or any vehicle for that matter switch your phone off before you start to drive. Our roads today carry much more traffic than they did in days gone by so therefore that means that we need much more concentration in our driving. If you answer your phone by holding the phone to your ear while you are driving you are breaking the law and

Driving On Motorways

your mind is on the person you are talking to and the conversation you are having so how can you concentrate on your driving at the same time.

While you are using your phone you need one hand to hold it which means that you are steering with one hand which is extremely dangerous and I think any Police Officer would pull you over for that. Think of yourself driving on a Motorway at 70mph in heavy traffic this is where you need your concentration most and here you are steering with one hand on the wheel and speaking to someone on your phone and quite possibly discussing a very complicated situation, your mind is on the conversation and not on your driving so you can't be classed as a safe and responsible driver. It only takes one very slight lapse of concentration to be involved in an accident, or maybe the cause of it. The Police watch very closely for drivers using their phones whilst driving not just on Motorways but all roads so remember when you are driving keep your phones switched off and stay safe.

CHAPTER SEVEN
LANE DISCIPLINE

As we are aiming this book mainly at the newly qualified driver, we will be using the Mirror-Signal-Manoeuvre-Position-Speed-Look routine which the Highway Code advises us to use, this should still be fresh in the new driver's mind, but it will also give the more experienced drivers a bit of a refresher, a manoeuvre is a planned movement. Each time we change lanes we must check our mirrors which means not only the interior mirror but also the two exterior side mirrors as well because we must know at all times what is happening not only to the front but also down both of our vehicle. When we want to move out from lane one we first of all check all our mirrors to see if it is safe to give a signal, we would not give a signal if

Fully Instructional

another driver was just starting to overtake us would we?, we should always give a signal for any manoeuvre on a Motorway because the traffic pattern changes so quickly, we may think we know what is happening but sometimes we may miss something then you think to yourself where did he come from so always play safe and give a good clear signal.

Not forgetting our right shoulder check into our blind spot, if lane two is clear especially to the rear and there isn't any drivers in lane three with a nearside signal on wishing to move back to lane two we will give a right hand signal, telling all other road users what our intentions are, we must bear in mind that the signal we give does not give us any right to move it only warns other drivers of our intentions and when we are sure it is safe we move smoothly into lane two. If we want to move to lane three we follow the same procedure as we did in lane one, moving from lane three back to lane two we do exactly the same to move back not forgetting to check that there is no other driver moving out of lane one at the same time as we are moving out of lane three, if that were to be the case which is quite possible we would both meet in lane two causing an accident so you can see how easily accidents happen just because drivers don't take enough time to look.

Driving On Motorways

At this point I would like to point out that when giving a signal we must give other road users time to react to it, we must not signal and move at the same time as many drivers do. When driving on Motorways we must give other drivers more time to react to our signals than when driving on other major roads because of the high speeds involved and sometimes heavier volumes of traffic, the traffic pattern changes so quickly so more time is needed, when you are making a manoeuvre do it smoothly and gently, this will also help to reduce Road Rage. Remember we are using a three lane Motorway so there is no such thing as a fast lane or a slow lane, speed does not determine the use of lanes. There are two ways to describe lanes on a Motorway and the first one is, the lane on the left next to the hard shoulder we could call the nearside lane, the next one we could call the centre lane obviously and the next lane next to the central reservation we could call that one the offside lane but not the fast lane. An easier way to identify the lanes from left to right is to simply call them lanes one two and three. From now on we shall always refer to the lane next to the hard shoulder as lane one. When we are driving on a Motorway, we should always use lane one for normal driving, lane two and three are used for overtaking, most of the time though lane one is occupied by L. G. Vs as their maximum speed is only

Fully Instructional

60mph and they are not allowed to use lane three so that is why we usually find them in lane one except when they are overtaking, if the were allowed in lane three, because they are slower they would restrict the flow of traffic on the Motorway.

We must remember that they have only two lanes to use and if we sit in lane two from one end of the Motorway to the other this prevents the L.G.Vs from overtaking at all and they have a days work to do with ferries to catch etc. Motorways were designed and built to get traffic from A to B faster and easier but to enable them to work to their maximum efficiency they must have rules and regulations and they can all be found in your current Highway Code. Poor lane discipline is a bad example of driving and can be the cause of many accidents, so this is why forward planning is so important, last minute lane changing is so dangerous because other drivers don't have time to react to it as it causes them to brake late and so we get a chain reaction all the way back down the carriageway.

To change lanes safely, only change one lane at a time because the traffic pattern changes so quickly that you just can't plan to change two lanes at the same time safely although we sometimes see drivers who have not been concentrating and nearly missing their junction turn off coming out of lane three, cutting right across

Driving On Motorways

the whole carriageway and actually exiting from the Motorway, complete madness.

Should you find yourself in that position, don't take any drastic measures like that, just carry on to the next junction and go back down the Motorway until you find your intended exit, much safer especially for the new driver. I would suggest that going on a Motorway for the first time you should just go from one junction to the next and then come off and park up somewhere safe to recap on what you have just done and to see what you think of it. After that build up your experience gradually it is far better than doing a long journey at the very start, you will enjoy it better that way.

CHAPTER EIGHT
OVERTAKING AND
MAKING PROGRESS

The overtaking manoeuvre is one of the most hazardous and dangerous situations that you are likely to encounter throughout the whole of your driving career so we must make sure that we know how it is carried out safely. Overtaking on major A roads with two way traffic is more dangerous than overtaking on dual-carriageways or Motorways because we have the oncoming traffic to deal with whereas on the Motorways and dual-carriageways we don't, as the traffic flow is all going in the same direction. We are covering overtaking on Motorways in this chapter and this can be very dangerous unless it is carried out in a safe and proper manner. Only overtake on the right don't use a lane to

Fully Instructional

your left for overtaking unless traffic is congested and you are already in that lane and the traffic on your right is moving slower than you are but do not change lanes to do this, you must also never use the hard shoulder for overtaking.

Overtaking on Motorways is not as difficult as overtaking on major A roads because we have a lot less hazards to contend with but having said that we still need a lot of attention, decision making and information about the traffic pattern before we carry out this manoeuvre. Before going into overtaking lets first talk a little about making progress, especially on Motorways as they are designed for fast flowing traffic, that is why they are nearly always straight, if there are any bends you will find that they are only very slight ones as this allows traffic to flow more freely. You will only find the occasional sharp bend where Motorways merge with each other, these sharp bends are purposely built for safety to make traffic slow down before merging. The speed limit is 70mph unless road signs tell us otherwise and you will find that traffic is usually travelling at that speed, sometimes more, so if you decide that you only want to travel at 60mph you then become a hazard to other road users because every vehicle that catches you up in your lane has to pull out and overtake you because you are in their way. Think of a journey that takes lets

Driving On Motorways

say three hours by Motorway and you drive at 60mph all the way just think of all the overtaking you have caused all the traffic because you are only travelling at 60mph. When a speed limit says70mph, providing road and traffic conditions allow you should drive at that speed and make progress especially if all the other traffic is. Remember we said earlier that overtaking is different on Motorways, and easier than on major A roads because we have the traffic flowing in the same direction so we don't have to consider any oncoming traffic or road junctions, roundabouts, pedestrian crossings and traffic lights but we still have some very serious hazards to deal with, the reason they are so serious is that the traffic is moving very fast so your decision making has to be early and very precise, needing a lot of attention why we must tell all other drivers early what our intentions are because the traffic pattern changes very quickly and traffic comes up from very quickly and it is sometimes difficult to judge their speed. We are now making good progress in lane one, travelling at 70mph so we are roughly 70 metres behind the slower vehicle in front when we decide to overtake, so that we can carry on making good progress, this is the stage at which we should start our overtaking manoeuvre so that we have got time and space to do it in.

Fully Instructional

The first thing we do is to check our mirrors to get a good view to the sides and rear to see whether it is safe and then make sure lane two is clear not only to the front but also to the rear because this is one of the danger points, traffic will be coming up on you very quickly, we know it shouldn't but traffic seem to want to drive at more than the speed limit these days, another important point is to make sure that there is no vehicles in lane three with a nearside indicators on because there could be a vehicle there deciding to move to the left at the same time as we decide to move to the right, if it is still safe and we have got the room we then give a good well timed signal to tell other road users what our intentions are giving them time to react to it, check the mirrors again and if it is still safe give a right shoulder check into our blind spot and move smoothly into lane two checking our mirrors again as you must always check your mirrors before any change of speed or direction for safety. It is no good driving right up to the vehicle in front like most drivers do because you have not got enough vision to the front especially if it's a L.G.V. or a coach and it also means that you have got to pull out abruptly which means that other drivers are not sure of your actions so why not start early and carry out your manoeuvre smoothly.

Driving On Motorways

As we are overtaking the slower traffic we are constantly checking the traffic in our mirrors, what are we looking for, do the vehicles we are overtaking want to overtake, is any other road user overtaking us and is lane one clear for us to move back into?, these are the things we should be asking ourselves all the time so you can see how much attention we must give our driving. When it is practical we will move back into lane one, sometimes we may have to drive miles before this can happen it just depends on how heavy the traffic is. To move back into lane one we check our mirrors because we could possibly have traffic on both sides of us, give a good well timed left signal check our mirrors again not forgetting our left shoulder check and if it is safe we move smoothly into lane one again checking our mirrors before we continue making sure that our signal has cancelled itself the reason I mention this is because a lot of drivers take it for granted that the self cancelling device will always cancel them for us but sometimes that is not the case. Either signal may sometimes stay on depending on the manoeuvre we have made and if this is the case we are driving along with a signal still on that we are not aware of and all other road users think we are going to do something that we have no intentions of doing so that creates total confusion, and you can see the dangers of this, it is what we call a forgotten signal

Fully Instructional

and we often see them and all you can put it down to is bad driving.

Whenever you finish a manoeuvre you should always check that your signal has cancelled, if they haven't then you must cancel them manually, when driving on major A roads we sometimes don't signal if we are sure that there is no one there, we call them unnecessary signals but on Motorways I strongly recommend that we signal all the time because of speed and volume of traffic if we all put safety before everything we can't go far wrong. When we read about overtaking, the books always tell us that when we have overtaken our intended vehicle we must not cut straight back in but they never tell us why. For example, when we are following other vehicles, lets say that we are travelling at 70mph making good progress we keep our overall stopping distance of roughly 70 metres away from them for safety, so if you consider the driver of the vehicle you are overtaking they are or should keep their overall stopping distance from the other traffic, so if we come along and cut straight in front of the vehicle we have just overtaken we have taken their overall stopping distance away from them and that puts them into immediate danger because they now have nowhere to go, no overall stopping distance to stop in if an emergency arises through no fault of their own.

Driving On Motorways

We see so many drivers who after overtaking cut straight in when there is miles of empty carriageway ahead of them it just does not make sense I don't think that they are conscious of the fact that they are doing it so that is the reason why we must not cut in after overtaking. Still on overtaking, when we want to overtake slower traffic in lane two so that we can travel at our own comfortable cruising speed we carry out the same procedure as we did in lane one when we first started overtaking. Mirror-Signal-Manoeuvre-Position Speed-look, when it is safe we smoothly ease our way into lane three, no sudden erratic movements as that makes other drivers unsure of your actions, so the key word is smoothly. Lane three is not the fast lane (no such thing as a fast or slow lane) it is an overtaking lane, we just have lane one for normal driving and the rest are for overtaking. After overtaking the slower traffic in lane two we then prepare to move back into lane two, we carry out our M.S.M.P.S.L. routine again not forgetting our left shoulder check because that can be a life saver especially if someone is driving in your blind spot, when safe we move back into lane two again. You may be thinking to yourself, why not move straight back to lane one from lane three if there is no traffic there but we can't because the traffic moves too quickly and we just have not got the time to do it safely so that

Fully Instructional

is why we can only change lanes one at a time. We have now returned to lane two with plans to return to lane one if it is convenient to do so, do not stay in lane two continuously as that is bad driving and it interrupts the traffic flow.

Never use the hard shoulder for overtaking unless directed to by the Police and only overtake if it is necessary, as we said earlier it is a very dangerous manoeuvre on a Motorway and even more so on major A roads as there are more hazards to contend with so why not be the good driver who is cool calm and collected and just go with the flow, that way you stand a much better chance of arriving at your destination safely. When you have finished reading this chapter I hope that you can see why it is so important that before setting out on your journey you must make sure that you are well rested as you can see how much concentration is needed.

CHAPTER NINE
APPROACHING JUNCTIONS AND SERVICE AREAS

Motorway junctions and Service Areas are places where traffic leaves and join Motorways, so as we approach them there is quite a lot of changes in the traffic pattern, drivers are changing lanes and overtaking so we usually see quite a lot of activity at these places. We get drivers who have not been concentrating on their driving and have left things very late for changing lanes to exit the Motorway, this causes traffic to start slowing down and this can be very dangerous so we must always be watching out for them. All this is happening in fast traffic so you can see how much attention this needs and how fit and fresh we must be for concentrating.

Fully Instructional

We will talk about approaching junctions first, Motorway driving can become very monotonous and can cause driving fatigue to set in, to combat this we must have plenty of fresh air circulating around the inside of the vehicle to keep us fresh and to keep our concentration levels high.

We must not allow anything to distract us from our driving, for instance if we have children in the car make sure that they have plenty of books to read and games to play with as they can be a big distraction to the driver when they are arguing and fighting. Another very important point to mention is the family pet, if you have any animals at all in the car please make sure that they are suitably restrained as the distraction of the driver would be enormous if we had a loose animal running around in the car. We always connect the colour blue to Motorways so when we are approaching a Motorway junction the first thing we see is a big blue sign, telling us that the next junction is one mile away. So we now have to prepare ourselves for exiting, if this is the case, you might think that a mile is a long way but you will find that it is not the case because of the speed you are travelling, the signs give us plenty of time to prepare so you can see the importance of time and space. On this mile marker sign it will have the junction number in the left hand bottom corner so that means that you can do a

Driving On Motorways

count down to your junction as you travel along, it also gives you the road numbers that you may need if you were leaving the Motorway at this junction.

The next sign that you will see is a similar sign telling you that the junction is half a mile away, it will still be showing the junction number but now, it not only tells you the road numbers it also tells you the names of the towns or cities you may be visiting. You will notice that lets say for instance you are in lane three overtaking when you see your junction coming up you have half a mile to move into lane one because if you are exiting at this junction you should be in lane one by the time you reach the half mile marker, if you are then you have time to prepare you exit comfortably. You can find all these signs in your Highway Code, which I suggest you do before starting your journey then you know what you are looking for. If for any reason you were to miss your junction for exiting you must not stop on the hard shoulder or reverse back, or try to make a "U" turn, you must carry on to the next junction before leaving the Motorway, sometimes a junction may be closed for road works and if it is and it's the one you want then the same thing applies, you must carry on to the next junction. Another good example of how you must be fully focussed on your driving because if you are not, it not only puts you in danger but it can also make your

Fully Instructional

journey become more expensive in time and fuel. As we pass the count down markers and slip road for exiting our next hazard will be any traffic merging on to the Motorway from the other side of the junction. You can usually see the traffic on the slip road long before you get there but not always, if there is traffic on the slip road wanting to join the Motorway then we should, being good courteous drivers as we are move into lane two if it is safe to do so letting the merging traffic into lane one, we must not force our way into lane two, if we can't move over safely we must stay where we are as we are the traffic with priority and the merging traffic will have to give way to us. It is nice to move over to let them in as we should all share the road with each other if we can, that way it keeps us all in a good frame of mind and feeling good, that in turn reduces that dreaded word road rage. Approaching Service Areas is very much the same as approaching junctions except that you get a much earlier mileage warning of them coming up. Be careful of other drivers suddenly deciding at the last minute that they want to use the Services as they may suddenly cut across your path to get into the Services, its wrong also very dangerous but it does happen. I would suggest that you use them quite often as they can sometimes be a very long distance apart and it can be very uncomfortable if you need the toilets or food plus

Driving On Motorways

the fact that, as the driver it is good to get out and stretch your legs every now and then. Another very important thing is, when you come out of the Services, before you get into your vehicle don't forget to walk round it and do that external check, you never know what you may find, do not forget to check your fuel before setting out again it is just the same procedure as when you first joined, you will join the Motorway from a slip road.

CHAPTER TEN
DEALING WITH ROADWORKS

When we see the "Road Works Ahead" sign which is a yellow sign with red, white and black markings on we think of hold-ups prolonging our journey and making us late on arrival at our destination, but this need not be the case. Remember the good driver, cool calm and collected, when planning the journey, like we said earlier we allowed extra time for things such as road works and other possible delays so when the traffic starts slowing down and building up we don't suffer any stress because we allowed for hold-ups and can mentally deal with it. If you look out of your window and look at some of the other drivers they are sitting there about six inches away from the bumper of the

Fully Instructional

vehicle in front tapping their fingers on the wheel full of frustration because this hold-up will make them late for their appointments etc simply because they didn't prepare.

We get good early warning signs of the road works ahead so that means that we have time to move into our correct lanes early and this also means that we have extra work to do because there are now extra signs to see and follow depending on the extent of the road works. The lanes may be narrow and you may even find yourself having to cross the central reservation and drive up the other side of the carriageway with no barriers between you and the oncoming traffic only red cones, these situations are called contra flow systems, there may be slow moving vehicles working within the road works. Now I would like to point out another very important thing, that is pedestrians who are not allowed to walk on Motorways unless you are broken down and walking on the hard shoulder to reach the emergency telephones and if you are unfortunate enough to be doing that you should walk as far away from the traffic in lane one as possible.

When we are driving through the road works we have to look out for people working there, people walking about carrying signs and moving cones etc. Speed limits are another thing to consider, you will see

Driving On Motorways

reduced speed limits throughout the whole length of the contra flow system to reduce speed of the traffic for the safety of the workers there, these are speed limits inside red circles which, if you read your Highway Code you will see that they are mandatory and must be adhered to as the Police will be keeping a very close eye on you. When road works have to be carried out we have to have some exceptions to the rules to enable things to work, one of them is the pedestrian we have just covered and now we have anothe,which is the hard shoulder. We shall be covering the hard shoulder later but the lay out of some road works means that we may have to use it as a lane, all the lanes are marked out with cones so all you have to do is to follow the signs, keep to the speed limits and remain fully focussed on your driving. As we leave the road works we must wait until we have passed the national speed limit sign before increasing our speed again.

CHAPTER ELEVEN
DRIVING IN ADVERSE WEATHER CONDITIONS

When driving in adverse weather conditions we have got to take everything into account, including the condition of the driver, vehicle, road surface, visibility and volume of the traffic so your attention and concentration and decision making becomes much harder. One of the most important things is your grip on the road surface, your visibility, braking, steering and acceleration, everything must be done smoothly and gently and in good time, if you use your steering, brakes, accelerator or even the clutch harshly this affects the forces governing the vehicle and often causes the tyres to loose their grip on the road surface and if this

Fully Instructional

happens you have lost control of your vehicle, a danger not only to yourself but to all other road users.

Harsh acceleration or letting the clutch in too quickly causes wheel spin, which in turn loses grip. The clutch is the device that delivers power to the vehicle so when we want to move the vehicle we let the clutch in, we are delivering power to the drive shafts which in turn moves the vehicle. If we let the clutch in too fast we are delivering power to the car which is far too fast which makes the wheels spin too fast which means that they can't grip the road surface.

The art of good driving is like we said earlier to do everything smoothly and gently so if we let the clutch in slowly and smoothly the power is delivered to the vehicle which in turn makes the wheels turn slowly which gives them a better chance to grip the road surface, remember that the slower your wheels turn the better your grip will be. When you are driving on any slippery surface, remember what we have just said about delivering power to your vehicle, use your accelerator very sparingly and you will see that you are maintaining grip while other drivers may be sliding all over the place. We see this happen all too often, when a driver is on a slippery surface they give the vehicle far too much acceleration, the more acceleration the faster the wheels spin and the faster they spin the less chance

Driving On Motorways

they have of gripping, Harsh steering is another factor which can cause loss of control, when you are driving in a straight line, providing you have enough tyre tread depth your tyres are gripping the road in their normal manner, if we change direction remember the tyres have still got to maintain their grip on the road and if we steer harshly the tyres have not got time to grip so you can loose control. The word 'time' seems to be a very important word because it seems to appear in everything we do related to driving. Harsh braking is one of the most common causes of accidents, the harder we brake the quicker the wheels stop which means that they haven't got time to grip but if we brake early and progressively then the tyres have got time to grip, the slower the tyres are turning the better they grip, they have their maximum gripping power just before they stop turning.

You often hear drivers saying that an accident happened, it most likely didn't, nine times out of ten accidents are caused by drivers not using the controls properly. If you think of your vehicle as a piece of machinery and the driver is giving it instructions by using the controls, the vehicle will only do what the driver tells it to do so if the driver feeds the wrong instructions to the vehicle by not using the controls correctly it can't respond to those instructions so it goes

Fully Instructional

out of control, so the driver can't blame the vehicle or anything else (but they do) they can only blame themselves, accidents are mainly caused by bad driving. When you start braking think of the vehicle and allow it time to respond by braking early and progressively and you will feel the control that you have with the vehicle and this will make enjoy your driving even more, give the other drivers time to react, remember they need time to react themselves. Adjust your speed to that of the weather conditions, if the roads are wet we need at least double the safe following distance, it now becomes the four second gap and if there is snow or ice about the gap should be increased still further.

When we are driving on snow or ice we can usually see it on the road surface but if we are driving on black ice we can't see it so must be very wary of this, the first signs of black ice will be if the road surface looks normal and suddenly your steering starts to feel very light it means that you are now driving on a very thin film of transparent ice between the road surface and the face of your tyres which means that your grip is very minimal. What you should do now is to check your mirrors and decelerate very slowly, take the power away slowly to give the vehicle to slow down gently any sudden movements may cause you to skid. Another good sign of black ice when we are driving on a good

Driving On Motorways

dry surface you can usually hear a slight noise from the tyres, but when you are on black ice there is no noise at all so when you are driving along and suddenly everything goes quiet, beware. When driving in fog especially on Motorways your visibility is greatly reduced so it becomes harder to see other vehicles especially the ones that have forgotten to put their lights on, we should always drive on dipped headlights whether in daylight or dark, it is no longer safe in this day and age to drive on side lights as the volume of traffic has greatly increased so we must use dipped headlights as our minimum lighting in any situation where visibility is reduced. This is not so that we can see, it is for other drivers to see us more easily, also if the visibility is reduced to less than100 metres we can use our rear fog lights so that other drivers can see us earlier and keep their distance. Rear fog lights are high intensity lights which are brighter than your rear side lights, they can pierce the fog better but beware when following traffic that's using them as they can sometimes make it harder to see their brake lights, these lights are designed only for fog, if you use them in any other situation they dazzle other drivers that may be following and always remember to switch them off after use or you will be breaking the law for using them when visibility is clear. Windy conditions can also be very

Fully Instructional

dangerous especially on Motorways as they are often long stretches of open carriageway that has very strong crosswinds on them. In these conditions it is better not to overtake unless you have to but if you have to be very careful especially large vehicles, if you are overtaking a large vehicle in a strong cross wind remember you are both pushing against the wind when you go under a fly-over or bridge there is suddenly no wind so there could be unusual movements and also beware of coming out from under the fly-over and hitting the wind again. As you gain experience in your driving (you can't buy experience you can only earn it) you will be more aware of all these hazards but for your first journey these are some of the things to be aware of.

When you are overtaking other vehicles you are shaded to a certain extent by those vehicles and as you pass them you can experience very strong cross winds which can blow you off course if you are not expecting it, especially if you have your roof rack loaded with luggage which makes your vehicle higher so the wind has more to push at so if you feel uncomfortable with the windy conditions slow down, you should also be aware of other vehicles being blown into your path. Whilst we are talking about luggage in your roof rack, if anything should fall on to the carriageway do not stop and try to retrieve it as it is far too dangerous, plus the fact that you

Driving On Motorways

will be breaking the law, you must carry on and stop at the next emergency telephone on the hard shoulder and report it to the Police Bad weather is nearly always blamed for causing accidents but that is not always the case, drivers cause most of the accidents themselves simply because they don't adjust their driving to the weather conditions and slow down. When we talk about bad weather and accidents we nearly always think of the winter months, if we have been lucky enough to have a long dry spell during the summer months a lot of drivers don't give the road surface a second thought. Lets take the height of the holiday season for example when the volume of traffic is even greater, just think of all those rubber tyres pounding the road surface, there is bound to be a certain amount of fine rubber particles left on the road surface plus all the oil drips and brake fluid drips not to mention the dust that sticks to all this and accumulates, driving along you don't notice this but its there. As soon as we get the first shower of rain we must slow down because as the water hit's the road surface the whole carriageway becomes so dangerous you might just as well be driving on ice.

This is one of the most dangerous times during the summer months but a lot of drivers are not aware that this happens until it too late, so remember when you see the first drops of rain starting to appear on your

Fully Instructional

windscreen you must slow down and drop back and drive at a safe speed, think to yourself if I have to brake will my tyres be able to grip the road surface As those first drops of rain appear on your windscreen do not put your wipers on straight away because as you have been driving along dead flies gets squashed on to the glass and if you put your wipers on straight away your windscreen will badly smear up and your vision has been greatly reduced and this could be accident time so let your windscreen get as much water on it as you can without loosing vision before switching your wipers on then your screen will clear much quicker. After a while, it all depends on how fast it is raining, all the lubrication on the road surface gets washed off with all the vehicles passing over it so then things begin to get better but don't forget that you still have the hazard of wet road surface to deal with, remember the four second gap applies on wet roads.

CHAPTER TWELVE
DRIVING AT NIGHT

Night driving can become very tiring because you are putting extra strain on your eyes, plus the fact that driving through the night, your body has the natural tendency to shut down for sleep so you must make sure that you are fit and fresh before starting out. Generally, driving at night becomes easier as the volume of traffic dies down which makes it possible to reach your destination quicker and easier. Providing you stick to the rules you should not have any problems but having said that there is extra hazards to deal with. If you do decide to make your journey by night, before you start, you should make sure that all your light lenses and mirrors are clean and also make sure that your windscreen is clean both inside and out and while you are cleaning

Fully Instructional

the inside of your windscreen don't forget to clean the interior mirror as this is something that is very often forgotten and just think what an important part that mirror plays in your driving. If you can't visualise what has just been said think how many times you will be using it on your journey from start to finish. The reason that all glass must be kept clean is that at night if you have a dirty windscreen the lights from other vehicles dazzle you and greatly reduces your visibility and we all know how important good visibility is especially at night. When following other traffic at night always use dipped headlights, driving on main beam behind other vehicles not only dazzles the driver in front but very importantly it reduces their vision to the rear so you are putting them in danger, always remember, dipped headlights and keep a safe distance behind and then the drivers in front of you will be a lot safer and they will also appreciate your thoughtfulness. We did mention safe stopping distances earlier when we talked about the two second gap in good road and traffic conditions in daylight but that changes when driving at night.

We said that we must always be able to stop well within the distance we can see to be clear ahead, that means the distance we can see to be clear within the range of our headlights. Overtaking at night now becomes more difficult because if we have kept to the rules and

Driving On Motorways

all our mirrors and windows are clean we should have reasonably good vision to the sides and front but when we want to overtake at night, at night, when we are looking in our mirrors to see what traffic is coming up from behind before we move out it now becomes very difficult to judge the speed of traffic coming up from behind because all you can see is a pair of headlights so we must be extremely careful before we make any manoeuvre at all. This is where a very well timed signal is needed to tell other drivers what our intentions are, especially if it is your first time in the dark.

Driving is colour coded and what we mean by that is, we learn to recognise things by different colours, when driving in the dark we have green studs to mark the slip roads at the Motorway junctions and Service Areas, red reflective studs to our nearside which mark the edge of the hard shoulder from lane one, then we have white studs which mark lanes one and two and then we have amber studs to mark the central reservation. When driving along if there is any lane closures ahead we always get a good advanced warning giving us time to change lanes, for example if we see a red cross above the lane we are driving in we must move out of that lane to the next appropriate lane because the red cross means that the lane is closed from the red cross onwards, the same applies to any lane. If there is a

Fully Instructional

red cross showing in all three lanes it means that the Motorway is closed and no one is allowed to pass the red signs except emergency vehicles. If that should happen everyone must stay in their vehicles as pedestrians are not allowed to walk on the carriageways and this also applies to daytime driving.

If you must drive at night make sure you see the weather reports before deciding to go because if you consider what we have just talked about in the last chapter about driving in bad weather, then we put all the extra hazards of night driving on top of that, consider things very carefully before setting out. I would not recommend anyone driving at night for the first Motorway trip, do it in daylight when life is much easier. So if you must make your journey at night in adverse weather conditions make sure you take plenty of hot drinks and warm blankets with you also a shovel in the boot for gritting, because if you are unfortunate enough to find the Motorway closed you could just sit there for some hours before moving again so always be prepared especially if you have children in the car.

CHAPTER THIRTEEN
BREAKDOWNS ON MOTORWAYS

Motorway driving puts extra stress and strain on your vehicle because you are driving at sustained high speeds for long periods of time, something that you don't normally do on major A roads so you have a greater chance of breaking down.

When you are driving along and you begin to hear unfamiliar sounds coming from your vehicle you should either pull in at the next Service Area or leave the Motorway at the next junction because breaking down on the Motorway can sometimes be very expensive. If you stop and think of the distance a breakdown vehicle may have to travel just to get to your stranded vehicle, it may have to travel miles up the other side of the

Fully Instructional

Motorway first, we know that most of the time you can't, but if you can it is not only safer but saves you money in the long run. If you are unfortunate enough to break down whilst travelling on the Motorway the first thing you must do is to put your hazard warning lights on and stop on the hard shoulder as near to an emergency telephone as possible, stopping as near to the left side of the hard shoulder as possible with your wheels turned to the left, it is very important that you leave your wheels in the left hand lock because if another vehicle hits you from behind your vehicle would get shunted further to the left, away from danger but if they were facing to the right your vehicle would get shunted on to the carriageway and just think how much trouble that would cause. The distance between a stationary vehicle on the hard shoulder and the passing traffic in lane one is very short and dangerous, just think of large juggernauts travelling at 60mph in lane one passing within a few feet of your vehicle, also if the driver is getting sleepy and drifting in lane one that distance could be even smaller so can you see the importance of putting as much distance as possible between your vehicle and the passing traffic in lane one. Always get out of the vehicle from the left hand side and make sure that all your passengers do the same as we have already pointed out the dangers if you don't, leave any animals that you may

Driving On Motorways

have in the vehicle but if you have to take them out say for fire, make sure that you keep them on leads and well away from the carriageway Get your passengers to sit on the bank side also well away from the carriageway, the reason for this is that if any other vehicle should run into the back of yours you would be in grave danger, its just not safe to sit in a vehicle that is standing on the hard shoulder. Do not use your warning triangle on the Motorway to warn other road users like you would on the major A roads, you must now find the nearest emergency telephone, they are situated at the back of the hard shoulder at one mile intervals along the hard shoulder, to find out which direction the nearest one is you will see small marker posts at the back of the hard shoulder with little arrows pointing to the nearest one. Never cross the central reservation hoping that there may be one on the other side as that is too dangerous plus the fact that you would be breaking the law. Always use the emergency telephones in preference to a mobile phone because then the emergency services can locate your exact location and can reach you quicker as all the emergency phones have location numbers on them and that is the first thing that the Police will want to know. If you use your mobile phone the first thing the Police will ask is for your exact location so that they know where to send a break down vehicle to. And if you have

Fully Instructional

been travelling for miles without passing a junction or a service area how can you identify your location to be reached. When you use emergency telephones you don't have to worry about not having the right change or dialling numbers in the dark you just simply pick up the receiver and you are automatically connected to the Police. The Police will ask you for the number stamped on the telephone box and they will identify your location straight away. Make sure that you know your registration number when doing this, the Police will organise the help that you need. If you are disabled and can't walk to the phones display your HELP sign and wait to be rescued. If it is dark while you are waiting to be rescued do not stand at the back of your vehicle or let any of your passengers do so because you may be blocking your rear lights or hazard warning lights from traffic on the Motorway and nobody will know that you are there. When your problems have been solved and you are ready to go again don't forget to pick up the phone and tell the Police that you are moving then they will know that the hard shoulder is clear again, Before you move away don't forget to switch off your hazard warning lights, do not drive straight into lane one from stationary when you enter the carriageway, drive down the hard shoulder and pick up speed first, just imagine yourself driving along at 70mph in lane

Driving On Motorways

one and a vehicle suddenly drives on to the carriageway from stationary right into your path, where would you go?. When joining a Motorway from the hard shoulder drive along the hard shoulder and pick up speed, check your mirrors give a good clear signal, pick a safe gap in the traffic flow do a right shoulder check and ease yourself smoothly into lane one when it is safe to do so. Other traffic will see what you are doing and move over and let you in if they can.

The hard shoulder plays a very important part in Motorway safety, it must be kept clear at all times if it is possible, that's why you can only use it in an emergency. If you are standing on the hard shoulder and the Police arrive you must be able to justify your reason for being there and if you can't be prepared for the consequences. If you stop and think what the hard shoulder does, it allows vehicles to get out of the traffic flow when they have broken down, but very importantly it allows emergency vehicles to get to the front of the accidents as quickly as possible as people may be there dying. So my advice to you is don't stop on the hard shoulder unless you have no other option, its no good saying to the Police I needed the toilet as that's not a good enough excuse, all they will say is you should have gone before passing the last service area or pulled off the Motorway at the last junction. When you see the services signed up

Fully Instructional

you should check with your passengers before reaching them whether anyone wants to stop because once you are passed the services its too late.

CHAPTER FOURTEEN
LEAVING THE MOTORWAY

We are nearly finished our journey by Motorway now, we have covered most aspects of using a Motorway in the daylight and in the dark so now all we have to do is leave the Motorway. Like we said earlier, we have been counting the junction numbers and we know that the next junction will be the one that we want to exit the Motorway. When we first see the sign it informs us that our junction is one mile away, the next sign tells us that our junction is half a mile away and by this time we should be in lane one ready for exiting. The next signs that we see is the count down markers to the slip road, there are three signs, they will have bars on them and each bar represents one hundred yards, this is the only

Fully Instructional

time you will see measurements in yards. The first sign has three bars so obviously this tells us that the slip road is three hundred yards away, the second sign has two bars and the third has one bar.

To leave the Motorway we start our manoeuvre at the first count down marker, this is where we check our mirrors and signal left to tell other drivers that we intend to leave the Motorway at this junction. All the other road users now have three hundred yards in which to react to our intentions, this is a very good example of a well timed signal, the next point is very important because unless we are controlled by the speed of the traffic in front of us, we must not decelerate while we are still on the carriageway because if we do, that makes all the other traffic behind either slow down or pull out to overtake us.

We must maintain our speed until we get to the slip road because that is the place to loose all our unwanted speed. The next sign is two hundred yards and then one hundred yards and we then move onto the slip road check our mirrors then decelerate to meet our new road, as we are on the slip road we must keep checking the speedometer as we may be travelling faster than we think we are. Remember that there will be two lanes on the slip road so when you actually leave the carriageway select your correct lane immediately depending on

Driving On Motorways

which direction you are taking as some slip roads are shorter than others, forward planning saves you lane changing when you may not have the time. Some slip roads have very sharp bends built in to them to make traffic slow down. so you must be aware of this, when we are driving on the major A roads it will take a little time to adjust to the different speeds and conditions so extra concentration is needed. You can see now what a big difference there is to driving on Motorways as to driving on the major A roads. Throughout this whole Motorway journey I have explained the importance of time and space. I hope you can see how much easier and safer it is and if you apply it to all your driving you should enjoy a safe and confident career.

About the Author

I am 68 years old, retired, Advanced Driving Instructor Trainer, I am separated from my wife and lived on my own for the last 15 years, driven on the roads ever since I was old enough to drive. When I first started, screen washer bottles had not been invented nor the flashing indicator system invented. I was a long distance lorry driver. When I was 43 I decided to change my career and become a Driving Instructor, I taught people to drive for a few years and then I decided to take a course in advanced driving instruction and teaching and passed at Diploma level so I then started training driving instructors which I really enjoyed. I took driving instructor training into a training college and was training classes of 25 pupils at a time employing 2 instructors right up to retiring age. Being retired with nothing to do all day I have decided to write about my work. My book "Driving On Motorways" should have been written years ago in my opinion as there is nobody on the market telling us how to drive safely on Motorways and I feel that it will be a success.

Printed in Great Britain
by Amazon